GAO
Accountability · Integrity · Reliability
Highlights

Highlights of GAO-10-523, a report to congressional requesters

I0500630

DEFENSE ACQUISITIONS

Navy's Ability to Overcome Challenges Facing the Littoral Combat Ship Will Determine Eventual Capabilities

Why GAO Did This Study

The Navy's Littoral Combat Ship (LCS) is envisioned as a reconfigurable vessel able to meet three missions: surface warfare, mine countermeasures, and anti-submarine warfare. It consists of the ship (seaframe) and the mission package it carries and deploys. The Navy plans to invest over $25 billion through fiscal year 2035 to acquire LCS. However, recurring cost growth and schedule delays have jeopardized the Navy's ability to deliver promised LCS capabilities.

Based on a congressional request, GAO (1) identified technical, design, and construction challenges to completing the first four ships within current cost and schedule estimates, (2) assessed the Navy's progress developing and fielding mission packages, and (3) evaluated the quality of recent Navy cost analyses for seaframes and their effect on program progress. GAO's findings are based on an analysis of government and contractor-generated documents, and discussions with defense officials and key contractors. This product is a public version of a For Official Use Only report, GAO-10-1006SU, also issued in August 2010.

What GAO Recommends

GAO recommends the Secretary of Defense take actions to ensure more realistic cost estimates, timely incorporation of design changes, and coordination of seaframe and mission package acquisition. The Department of Defense concurred with each of these recommendations.

View GAO-10-523 or key components. For more information, contact Belva Martin at (202) 512-4841 or martinb@gao.gov.

What GAO Found

The Navy faces technical, design, and construction challenges to completing the first four seaframes within current cost and schedule estimates. The Navy and its shipbuilders have learned lessons from construction of the first two seaframes that have positioned them to more effectively construct future vessels. However, technical issues with the first two seaframes have yet to be fully resolved. Addressing these technical issues has required the Navy to implement design changes at the same time LCS 3 and LCS 4 are being built. Incorporating changes during this phase will likely require additional labor hours beyond current forecasts. Together, these challenges may hinder the ability of shipbuilders to apply lessons learned to follow-on ships and could undermine anticipated benefits from recent capital investments in the LCS shipyards.

Challenges developing mission packages have delayed the timely fielding of promised capabilities, limiting the ships' utility to the fleet during initial deployments. Until these challenges are resolved, it will be difficult for the Navy to align seaframe purchases with mission package procurements and execute planned tests. Key mine countermeasures and surface warfare systems encountered problems in operational and other testing that delayed their fielding. For example, four of six Non-Line-of-Sight Launch System missiles did not hit their intended targets in recent testing, and the Department of Defense has since canceled the program. Further, Navy analysis of anti-submarine warfare systems has shown the planned systems do not contribute significantly to the anti-submarine warfare mission. These combined challenges have led to procurement delays for all three mission packages. Mission package delays have also disrupted program test schedules—a situation exacerbated by early deployments of initial ships—limiting their availability for operational testing. In addition, these delays could disrupt program plans for simultaneously acquiring seaframes and mission packages. Until mission packages are proven, the Navy risks investing in a fleet of ships that does not deliver promised capability.

The Navy entered contract negotiations in 2009 for fiscal year 2010 funded seaframes with an incomplete understanding of LCS program costs. These contract negotiations proved unsuccessful, prompting the Navy to revise its acquisition strategy for the program. The contractors' proposals for construction of the next three ships exceeded the approximate $1.4 billion in funds the Navy had allocated in its fiscal year 2010 budget. In response, the Navy revised its strategy to construct one seaframe design instead of two for fiscal year 2010 ships and beyond in an effort to improve affordability. Navy cost analyses completed prior to the failed negotiations in 2009 lack several characteristics essential to a high-quality cost estimate. These characteristics include the completion of sensitivity and uncertainty analyses and an independent review of the cost estimate. The Navy plans to complete a more comprehensive cost estimate before award of additional ship contracts in 2010.

_____United States Government Accountability Office

Contents

Figures

United States Government Accountability Office
Washington, DC 20548

August 31, 2010

The Honorable Solomon Ortiz
Chairman
The Honorable J. Randy Forbes
Ranking Member
Subcommittee on Readiness
Committee on Armed Services
House of Representatives

The Honorable Gene Taylor
Chairman
The Honorable W. Todd Akin
Ranking Member
Subcommittee on Seapower and Expeditionary Forces
Committee on Armed Services
House of Representatives

The Navy's Littoral Combat Ship (LCS) is envisioned as a vessel able to be reconfigured to meet three different mission areas: mine countermeasures, surface warfare, and anti-submarine warfare. Its design concept consists of two distinct parts—the ship itself (seaframe) and the mission package it carries and deploys. The Navy currently plans to invest over $25 billion to acquire LCS seaframes and mission packages through fiscal year 2035. However, recurring cost growth and schedule delays in the program have jeopardized the Navy's ability to deliver promised LCS capabilities.

In light of these developments, you asked us to evaluate LCS planning and implementation efforts. In response to this request, we (1) identified technical, design, and construction challenges to completing the first four seaframes within current cost and schedule estimates; (2) assessed the Navy's progress developing and fielding mission packages; and (3) evaluated the quality of recent Navy cost analyses for seaframes and their effect on program progress. This product is a public version of a For Official Use Only report, GAO-10-1006SU, also issued in August 2010.

To identify challenges to completing the first four seaframes, we analyzed Department of Defense and contractor-generated documents that addressed technical challenges and cost and schedule performance for LCS seaframes including sea trial reports for the first two ships, construction progress briefings, and monthly contract performance reports. We corroborated this information through discussions with officials responsible for managing LCS design and construction activities including Navy program officials, technical authorities, and requirements officers; LCS prime contractors and shipbuilders; and the Office of the Secretary of Defense. To assess the Navy's progress developing and fielding mission packages, we reviewed documents that outline LCS mission package plans and performance including program schedules and recent test reports. We also held discussions with Navy program offices and Department of Defense agencies responsible for acquiring and testing key LCS mission systems to gather additional information on remaining risks to mission package development and integration. To evaluate the quality of recent Navy cost analyses, we compared the Navy's total ownership cost baseline estimate for the LCS program against the characteristics inherent in high-quality cost estimates as outlined in our cost estimating and assessment guide.[1] In addition, we interviewed LCS cost analysts and program officials to supplement our analysis and gain additional visibility into the Navy's process for developing its cost estimate. A more detailed description of our scope and methodology is presented in appendix I.

We conducted this performance audit from July 2009 to August 2010 in accordance with generally accepted government auditing standards. Those standards require that we plan and perform the audit to obtain sufficient, appropriate evidence to provide a reasonable basis for our findings and conclusions based on our audit objectives. We believe that the evidence obtained provides a reasonable basis for our findings and conclusions based on our audit objectives.

Background

LCS is designed to move fast and transport manned and unmanned mine countermeasures, surface warfare, and anti-submarine warfare systems into theater. For LCS, the seaframe consists of the hull; command and control systems; automated launch, handling, and recovery systems; and certain core combat systems like an air defense radar and 57-millimeter gun. The Navy is procuring the first four ships in two different designs from shipbuilding teams led by Lockheed Martin and General Dynamics. Lockheed Martin and General Dynamics currently build their designs at Marinette Marine and Austal USA shipyards, respectively. Figure 1 shows

---

[1]See GAO, *GAO Cost Estimating and Assessment Guide: Best Practices for Developing and Managing Capital Program Costs*, GAO-09-3SP (Washington, D.C.: Mar. 2009).

the first two LCS seaframes, USS Freedom (LCS 1) and USS Independence (LCS 2).

Figure 1: LCS Seaframes

USS Freedom (LCS 1)

USS Independence (LCS 2)

Sources: Lockheed Martin (left); General Dynamics (right).

Note: LCS 1 is a steel monohull while LCS 2 is an aluminum trimaran.

The Navy is embedding LCS's mine countermeasures, surface warfare, and anti-submarine warfare capabilities within mission packages. These packages are comprised of unmanned underwater vehicles, unmanned surface vehicles, towed systems, and hull- and helo-mounted weapons. Table 1 identifies the systems included in the LCS mission packages.

Table 1: Systems Included in the Baseline LCS Mine Countermeasures, Surface Warfare, and Anti-Submarine Warfare Mission Packages

Mine Countermeasures Mission Package	Surface Warfare Mission Package	Anti-Submarine Warfare Mission Package[a]
Airborne Laser Mine Detection System	MK 46 30-Millimeter Gun System	Multi-Function Towed Array
Airborne Mine Neutralization System	Non-Line-Of-Sight Launch System and Missiles[b]	Remotely Towed Active Source
AN/AQS-20A Sonar	Maritime Security Module	Multi-Static Off-Board Source
Remote Minehunting System		Remote Multi-Mission Vehicle
Coastal Battlefield Reconnaissance and Analysis System		Unmanned Surface Vehicle
Organic Airborne and Surface Influence Sweep System		Unmanned Surface Vehicle Dipping Sonar
Rapid Airborne Mine Clearance System		Unmanned Surface Vehicle Towed Array System
Unmanned Surface Vehicle with Unmanned Surface Sweep System		

Source: Navy.

Note: Aviation assets and support equipment including the MH-60R helicopter, MH-60S helicopter, MQ-8B Vertical Take-off and Landing Tactical Unmanned Aerial Vehicle, mission package computing environment, and stowage containers are not included.

[a]The Navy is evaluating new configurations for future anti-submarine warfare mission packages.

[b]The Navy planned to employ the Army's Non-Line-of-Sight Launch System and Missiles to provide LCS with a small boat engagement capability, but the program was canceled in May 2010 because of performance and cost problems. The Navy is evaluating alternative weapon systems to replace the Non-Line-of-Sight Launch System and Missiles.

Fundamental to the capability of the LCS seaframe is its ability to move quickly ahead of other ships and deploy its offboard sensors to secure lanes of transit. To deploy LCS's mine countermeasures and anti-submarine warfare systems, the Navy will rely extensively on (1) automated launch, handling, and recovery systems embedded in each seaframe and (2) helicopters and unmanned aerial vehicles. The Navy's acquisition approach is to populate initial versions of mission packages with a mixture of developmental and production-representative systems, gradually moving to all production-representative systems that constitute the baseline configuration for each package. The Navy plans to procure 55 seaframes and 64 mission packages (24 mine countermeasures, 24 surface warfare, and 16 anti-submarine warfare) as part of the LCS program.

The Navy has required LCS seaframes to meet Level 1 survivability standards. Ships built to Level 1 are expected to operate in the least severe environment, away from the area where a carrier group is operating or the general war-at-sea region. These vessels should also maintain good handling in bad weather—including seas above 30 feet high (sea state 8)[2]—and have systems for fighting fires on board the ships, hardening against electromagnetic pulses, and protection against chemical, biological, or radiological contamination. Unlike surface warships like cruisers and destroyers, Level 1 ships (including LCS) are not designed to maintain their mission capabilities after incurring substantive damage. Current ships in the fleet built to the Level 1 standard include material support ships, mine-warfare vessels, and patrol combatants.

Two broad categories of contract types are available for government procurements, including ship procurement: fixed-price and cost-reimbursement. Fixed-price contracts provide for a firm price or, in appropriate cases, an adjustable price that may include a ceiling price, a target price, or both. This contract type places the risk on the contractor, who generally bears the responsibility of increased costs of performance. Cost-reimbursement contracts provide for payment of allowable incurred costs, to the extent prescribed in the contract. This contract type places most of the risk on the government, which may pay more than budgeted should incurred costs be more than expected when the contract was signed.

The Navy awarded cost-reimbursable contracts for detail design and construction of the first two seaframes—LCS 1 and LCS 2—in December 2004 and October 2005 for $188.2 million and $223.2 million, respectively. It later exercised options on each of these contracts in June and December 2006 for construction of the third and fourth ships (LCS 3 and LCS 4). However, changing technical requirements, evolving designs, and construction challenges increased the government's estimated prices at completion for the LCS 1 and LCS 2 seaframes to about $500 million each. This cost growth precipitated concern within the Navy that similar outcomes were possible for LCS 3 and LCS 4. In response, the Navy reassessed program costs and structure, revisited the acquisition strategy for future ships, and entered into negotiations with its shipbuilders to convert the LCS 3 and LCS 4 contracts into fixed-price contracts. The Navy was unable to reach agreement with its shipbuilders on fixed-price terms

---

[2]The Navy classifies sea states on a scale of 0 to 9 depending on the roughness of the water as caused by wind or other disturbances. Sea states 0 to 3 represent calm to slight seas of 4 feet or less. Sea state 4 is characterized by moderate seas of 4 to 8 feet. Sea states 5 to 6 range from rough to very rough seas between 8 to 20 feet. Sea states 7 to 9—the most challenging marine conditions—reflect high to extremely rough seas, including seas above 20 feet.

for these ships, subsequently leading the Navy to terminate, in part, the LCS 3 and LCS 4 contracts in April and November 2007 for the convenience of the government. In March and May 2009, the Navy awarded new fixed-price contracts for LCS 3 and LCS 4. According to the Navy, work completed and materials procured under the terminated original contract options for LCS 3 and LCS 4—totaling approximately $192 million—are not included in the current contract values for those ships.

In our work on shipbuilding best practices, we found that achieving design stability before start of fabrication is a key step that leading commercial shipbuilders and ship buyers follow to ensure their vessels deliver on-time, within planned costs, and with planned capabilities.[3] Leading commercial firms assess a ship design as stable once all basic and functional design activities have been completed. Basic and functional design refers to two-dimensional drawings and three-dimensional, computer-aided models (when employed) that fix the ship's hull structure; set the ship's hydrodynamics; route all major distributive systems including electricity, water, and other utilities; and identify the exact positioning of piping and other outfitting within each block of the ship. At the point of design stability, the shipbuilder has a clear understanding of both ship structure as well as ship electrical, piping, and other systems that traverse individual blocks of the ship. To achieve design stability, shipbuilders need suppliers (also called vendors) to provide complete, accurate system information prior to entering basic design. This vendor-furnished information describes the exact dimensions of a system or piece of equipment going into a ship, including space and weight requirements, and also requirements for power, water, and other utilities that will have to feed the system.

As is typical for all ships, the LCS construction phase includes several steps: block fabrication, assembly and outfitting of blocks, block erection, launch, and delivery. During block fabrication, metal plates are welded together into elements called blocks. Blocks are the basic building units for a ship, and when completed they will form completed or partial compartments, including accommodation space, engine rooms, and storage areas. Blocks are generally outfitted with pipes, brackets for

---

[3]See GAO, *Best Practices: High Levels of Knowledge at Key Points Differentiate Commercial Shipbuilding from Navy Shipbuilding*, GAO-09-322 (Washington, D.C.: May 13, 2009).

machinery or cabling, ladders, and any other equipment that may be available for installation at this early stage of construction. This allows a block to be installed as a completed unit when it is welded to the hull of the ship. Installing equipment at the block stage of construction is preferable because access to spaces is not limited by doors or machinery, unlike at later phases. Blocks are welded together to form grand blocks and then erected with other grand blocks in a drydock or, in the case of LCS, in a building hall. Finally, once the ship is watertight and the decision is made to launch—or float the ship in water—the ship is then towed into a quay or dock area where final outfitting and testing of machinery and equipment like main engines will occur. Afterwards, the ship embarks on sea trials where performance is evaluated against the contractually required specifications and overall quality is assessed. Following sea trials, the shipyard delivers the ship to the buyer.

LCS 1 was delivered to the Navy in September 2008, with LCS 2 following in December 2009. The Navy has also accepted delivery of five partial mission packages to date. Currently, LCS 1 is on deployment, LCS 2 is undergoing post-delivery work, and LCS 3 and LCS 4 remain in different stages of construction. In addition, development and testing activities for the mine countermeasures, anti-submarine warfare, and surface warfare mission packages continue. The Navy deployed LCS 1 two years ahead of its previous schedule and prior to the ship completing initial operational test and evaluation. The Navy also stated that early deployment is possible for LCS 2.

Initial operational test and evaluation is intended to assess a weapon system's capability in a realistic environment when maintained and operated by sailors, subjected to routine wear-and-tear, and employed in typical combat conditions against a simulated enemy who fights back. During this test phase, the weapon system is exposed to as many actual operational scenarios as possible—a process that reveals the weapon system's capabilities under stress. Once the fleet has attained the ability to effectively employ and operate the weapon system, initial operational capability is achieved.

Until September 2009, the Navy planned to continue buying both ship designs. In September 2009, the Navy announced it was revising the LCS program's acquisition strategy and would select one seaframe design before awarding contracts for any additional ships. In the National

Defense Authorization Act for Fiscal Year 2010, Congress mandated a $480 million cost cap for each LCS, starting with fiscal year 2011 funded seaframes.[4] In an effort to comply with this mandate, Navy officials have stated that a major program review (milestone B)—and completion of an independent cost estimate—will precede further contract awards in the program.

Cost estimates are necessary for government acquisition programs, like LCS, for many reasons: to support decisions about funding one program over another, to develop annual budget requests, to evaluate resource requirements at key decision points, and to develop performance measurement baselines. A cost estimate is a summation of individual cost elements, using established methods and valid data, to estimate the future costs of a program, based on what is known today. The management of a cost estimate involves continually updating the cost estimate with actual data as they become available, revising the estimate to reflect changes, and analyzing differences between estimated and actual costs—for example, using data from a reliable earned value management system.

Ongoing Development of Key Seaframe Systems Could Impede Efficient Construction of Initial Follow-On Ships

The Navy faces technical, design, and construction challenges to completing the first four seaframes within current cost and schedule estimates. The Navy and its shipbuilders have learned lessons from construction of the first two seaframes that can be applied to construction of future vessels. However, technical issues with the first two seaframes have yet to be fully resolved, posing risk of design changes to follow on ships already under construction. Addressing these technical issues has required the Navy to implement design changes at the same time LCS 3 and LCS 4 are being built. Incorporating changes during this phase may disrupt the optimal construction sequence for these ships, requiring additional labor hours beyond current forecasts. Together, these challenges may hinder the ability of shipbuilders to apply lessons learned to follow on ships and could undermine anticipated benefits from recent capital investments in the LCS shipyards.

---

[4]Pub. L. No 111-84, § 121 (c). Section 121(d) also authorizes the Secretary of the Navy to waive and adjust provisions of the cost limitation upon making certain findings and other conditions.

Cost Growth and Schedule Delays Have Hampered Construction of the First Four Ships

Initial LCS seaframes have required more funding and taken longer to construct than the Navy originally planned. The Navy has accepted delivery of the first two ships (LCS 1 and LCS 2), which, according to the Navy, reduces the likelihood of additional cost increases and schedule delays on those ships. Further, the Navy's decision to partially terminate, and later re-award, construction contracts for follow-on ships (LCS 3 and LCS 4) changed the planned delivery dates for those ships. Tables 2 and 3 highlight the cost growth and schedule delays associated with the first four ships of the class.

Table 2: Cost Growth on Initial LCS Seaframes

Dollars in millions

Ship	Initial budget	Fiscal year 2011 budget	Total cost growth	Cost growth as a percent of initial budget
LCS 1	$215.5	$537.0	$321.5	149.2%
LCS 2	$256.5	$607.0[a]	$350.5	136.6%
LCS 3-4	$1,260.7[b]	$1,357.7	$97.0	7.7%

Source: GAO analysis of President's budget data.

Note: Fiscal year 2011 budget figures identified for LCS 1 and LCS 2 exclude funding associated with certain design, planning, and program management activities for these ships. These funds total $170.0 million and $177.0 million for LCS 1 and LCS 2, respectively.

[a] Total excludes Department of Defense reprogramming actions in July 2010 that added $5.256 million in funding to complete post-delivery work on LCS 2.

[b] Initial budget figure for LCS 3 and LCS 4 reflects the total Shipbuilding and Conversion, Navy (SCN) funds the Navy requested in fiscal year 2009 to construct two LCS seaframes plus the value of funds and materials applied from the two canceled, fiscal year 2006 funded LCS seaframes. Congress originally appropriated $440 million in fiscal year 2006 to construct these two ships

Table 3: Delays in Delivering Initial LCS Seaframes

Ship	Initial planned delivery date	Current estimated/actual delivery date	Total construction delays
LCS 1	January 2007	September 2008	20 months
LCS 2	October 2007	December 2009	26 months
LCS 3	November 2012	February 2012	N/A
LCS 4	January 2013	April 2012	N/A

Source: GAO analysis of President's budget data.

Note: Initial planned delivery dates for LCS 3 and LCS 4 reflect the planned schedules for two fiscal year 2009 funded LCS seaframes. Previously, the Navy funded these two ships in fiscal year 2006 and expected deliveries in October 2008. The Navy's decision to partially terminate construction contracts for the two fiscal year 2006 ships, coupled with Congress's decision to rescind appropriations for one fiscal year 2008 funded seaframe, account for several months of schedule gains realized for LCS 3 and LCS 4.

First Two Seaframes Delivered to the Fleet, but Technical Challenges Currently Limit Their Capabilities

The Navy accepted delivery of LCS 1 and LCS 2 with both seaframes in an incomplete state and with outstanding technical issues. After experiencing significant cost increases and schedule delays on these ships, the Navy judged it more cost efficient to accept the incomplete ships and resolve remaining issues post-delivery. According to Navy officials, this step afforded the Navy more control over remaining work and provided the ability to use repair yards that charge less than the builder in some instances. Although the ships are currently in service, the Navy continues to address technical issues on each seaframe. Addressing these issues has required the Navy to schedule extensive post-delivery work periods for each ship, which were not fully anticipated at the time of lead ship contract awards. For instance, to resolve the LCS 1 issues, the Navy allocated several months for two industrial post-delivery availability periods in 2009. A similar schedule is planned for LCS 2.

The Navy has made significant progress resolving LCS 1 deficiencies. While challenges with several systems were identified at delivery, the Navy deferred testing of other systems until after delivery. The shipbuilder had not completed installation of several LCS 1 systems prior to delivery, contributing to Navy decisions to defer key elements of the ship's acceptance trials until later.[5] Most notably, the Navy deferred testing of the ship's launch, handling, and recovery system—a system instrumental to deploying and recovering mission package elements that, if not performing adequately, will impair LCS capability. To date, a full demonstration of this system remains incomplete. Navy simulations to date have identified risks in safely launching and recovering mission systems that experience pendulous motion during handling—such as the remote multi-mission vehicle and unmanned surface vehicle systems. Navy officials stated, however, that the fleet successfully demonstrated operation and movement of an embarked 11-meter rigid-hull inflatable boat, having used one extensively for counterdrug operations in the Caribbean in March 2010.

Another challenge for LCS 1 launch, handling, and recovery is the potential for unacceptably high water levels during high sea states in the waterborne mission zone—the area at the stern end of the ship designed to launch watercraft through stern doors and down a ramp directly into the water. Further, LCS 1's launch, handling, and recovery system has also

---

[5]In addition, Navy officials stated that environmental and treaty constraints prohibited testing of several ship systems within the confines of the Great Lakes.

experienced difficulty safely moving payloads on the ship. Most notably, payload handling cranes will not be installed until a future maintenance period in fiscal year 2013.

Like LCS 1, the Navy identified several significant technical deficiencies on LCS 2 during that ship's acceptance trials. However, because LCS 2 was only recently delivered (December 2009), the Navy remains in the early stages of addressing the issues facing that ship. Similar to LCS 1, the Navy chose to accept delivery of LCS 2 prior to the shipbuilder completing installation of key systems. The incomplete condition of the ship contributed to Navy decisions to defer key elements of acceptance trials until after delivery. As was the case with LCS 1, these deferments included testing of the LCS 2 launch, handling, and recovery system for mission watercraft.

LCS 2 is designed to employ a twin boom extensible crane system to launch, handle, and recover mission watercraft. This system includes the crane, synthetic lift lines, and a straddle carrier. The synthetic lift lines attach to the crane to retrieve watercraft, but remain an unproven, new capability to the Navy. Another risk to the system is the ability of the straddle carrier to interface with, maneuver, and return to stowage the rigid-hull inflatable boat, remote multi-mission vehicle, and unmanned surface vehicle systems—three of the largest watercraft the Navy plans to embark on LCS 2. According to the Navy, the straddle carrier was used to successfully move the remote multi-mission vehicle and unmanned surface vehicle during onboard trials in March 2010.

Continuing Design Changes Could Hinder Efficient Construction of LCS 3 and LCS 4

The Navy's efforts to resolve technical issues affecting LCS 1 and LCS 2, implement cost reduction measures, and increase mission capability have led to design changes for LCS 3 and LCS 4, several of which are not yet complete. These design changes have affected the configuration of several major ship systems for LCS 3 and LCS 4 including propulsion, communications, electrical, and navigation. The Navy is working to implement these design changes concurrent with LCS 3 and LCS 4 construction activities. Incorporating design changes on the lead seaframes while the follow-on ships are under construction may disrupt the optimal construction sequence for LCS 3 and LCS 4, requiring additional labor hours beyond current forecasts. As we have previously reported, by delaying construction start until basic and functional design is completed and a stable design is achieved, shipbuilders minimize the risk of design changes and the subsequent costly rework and out-of-sequence work these changes can drive.[6]

Benefits Derived from Recent Process Improvements and Capital Investments in the LCS Shipyards May Not Be Fully Realized on Early Follow-On Ships

The Navy and its shipbuilders learned valuable lessons from the construction of the lead ships that can save time and money on the construction of follow-on ships. The shipbuilding teams have implemented process improvements based on these lessons and made capital investments in their yards in an effort to increase efficiency. Despite the various improvements to capacity and processes at the shipyards, capitalizing on these improvements might be challenging given the significant design changes still occurring in the program. As technical issues are resolved on the lead seaframes, this, in general, leads to redesign—and potentially costly rework—for initial follow-on ships. Thus, while efficiencies will be gained as a result of the shipyards' improvement, remaining technical issues on the seaframes will likely continue to jeopardize the Navy's ability to complete the first four seaframes within planned cost and schedule estimates.

Mission Package Delays Limit Ship Capabilities in the Near Term and Pose Risk to Efficient Execution of Program Acquisition and Test Plans

Challenges developing and procuring mission packages have delayed the timely fielding of promised capabilities, limiting the ships' utility to the fleet during initial deployments. Until these challenges are resolved, it will be difficult for the Navy to align seaframe purchases with mission package procurements and execute planned tests. Key mine countermeasures and surface warfare systems have encountered technical issues that have delayed their development and fielding. Further, Navy analysis of LCS anti-submarine warfare systems found these capabilities did not contribute significantly to the anti-submarine warfare mission. These challenges have led to procurement delays for all three mission packages. For instance, key elements of the surface warfare package remain in development, requiring the Navy to deploy a less robust capability on LCS 1. Mission package delays have also disrupted program test schedules—a situation exacerbated by decisions to deploy initial ships early, which limit their availability for operational testing. In addition, these delays could disrupt program plans for simultaneously acquiring seaframes and mission

---

[6]See GAO, *Best Practices: High Levels of Knowledge at Key Points Differentiate Commercial Shipbuilding from Navy Shipbuilding*, GAO-09-322 (Washington, D.C.: May 13, 2009).

packages. Until mission package performance is proven, the Navy risks investing in a fleet of ships that does not deliver promised capability.

Challenges Developing LCS Mission Package Systems Have Delayed Their Planned Fielding Dates

Development efforts for most of these systems predate the LCS program—in some cases by 10 years or more. Recent testing of mission package systems has yielded less than desirable results. To date, most LCS mission systems have not demonstrated the ability to provide required capabilities. Further, the Navy has determined that an additional capability will be incorporated into future anti-submarine warfare mission packages. The existing anti-submarine warfare mission package procurement is temporarily suspended, and performance will be assessed during at-sea testing in 2010. In addition to the sensors, vehicles, and weapons included in each mission package, each LCS will rely on aircraft and their support systems to complete missions.

Mine Countermeasures

Mine countermeasures missions for LCS will involve detecting, classifying, localizing, identifying, and neutralizing enemy sea mines in areas ranging from deep water through beach zones.[7] We have previously reported on challenges the Navy faces in transitioning the mine countermeasures mission to LCS.[8] Figure 2 illustrates how the Navy plans to employ the LCS mine countermeasures systems against mine threats.

---

[7]While the Navy will use LCS systems to detect mines in the very shallow (40 feet to 30 feet water only), surf (less than 10 feet to 0 feet water), and beach zones, other military assets will neutralize these mines.

[8]See GAO, *Defense Acquisitions: Overcoming Challenges Key to Capitalizing on Mine Countermeasures Capabilities*, GAO-08-13 (Washington, D.C.: Oct. 12, 2007).

Figure 2: Operational Concept for LCS Mine Countermeasures Systems

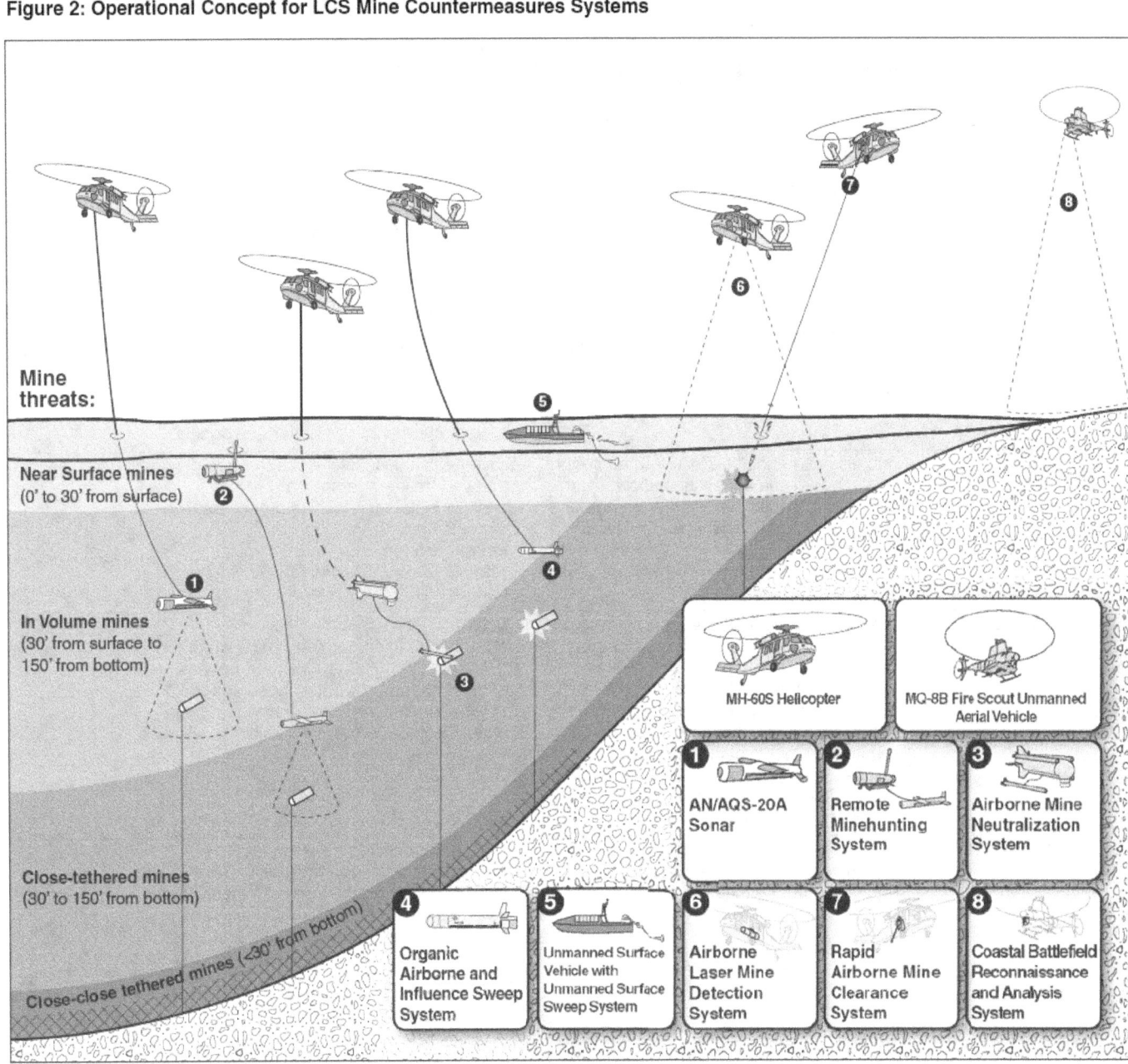

Source: GAO analysis of Navy data.

Table 4 shows the status of mine countermeasures mission package systems.

Table 4: Navy's Progress Developing and Fielding Mine Countermeasures Mission Package Systems

Mission system	Capabilities description	Development status	Estimated fielding date
AN/AQS-20A Sonar	Provides identification of bottom mines in shallow water and detection, localization, and classification of bottom, close-tethered, and volume mines in deep water	System has met performance requirements in developmental testing. Operational testing has been delayed, however, due to decertification of the system following integration problems with the common tow cable that connects it to the MH-60S helicopter.	2011
Airborne Laser Mine Detection System	Detects, classifies, and localizes floating and near-surface moored mines in deep water	System has demonstrated partial capability during developmental testing. Current challenges include the ability to detect mines at the required maximum depth or classify mines at surface depths.	2011
Airborne Mine Neutralization System	Identifies and neutralizes unburied bottom and moored sea mines in shallow water that are impractical or unsafe to counter using existing minesweeping systems	System has successfully streamed and deployed an inert neutralizer in developmental testing. The mount that connects the system to the MH-60S carriage, stream, tow, and recovery system is being redesigned following loss of a test unit.	2011
Coastal Battlefield Reconnaissance and Analysis System	Provides intelligence preparation of the battlefield information, which accurately depicts tactical objectives, minefields, and obstacles in the surf zone, on the beach, and through the beach exit during amphibious and expeditionary operations; future increments planned will provide active (day/night), surf zone, buried minefield detection, and real-time processing capabilities	System has demonstrated capability to detect buried mines on the beach when flown from the MH-53 helicopter, but has yet to be integrated with its host platform, the MQ-8B Vertical Take-off and Landing Tactical Unmanned Aerial Vehicle.	2012
Organic Airborne and Surface Influence Sweep System	Provides organic, high-speed magnetic/acoustic influence minesweeping capability where mine hunting is not feasible (adverse environmental conditions)	Engineering development model experienced excessive corrosion at its interface point with the common tow cable during testing from an MH-53E helicopter. The Navy has implemented a design solution, and new models are in production.	2012

Mission system	Capabilities description	Development status	Estimated fielding date
Remote Minehunting System	Underwater vehicle towing the AN/AQS-20A sonar used to detect, classify, locate, and identify minelike objects	The Navy abandoned initial operational test and evaluation of this system in June 2007 following reliability issues—both software and hardware related—affecting the underwater vehicle. Subsequent plans for resuming this testing in September 2008 were deferred because of continuing concerns about the reliability of the underwater vehicle, and the scheduled test was downgraded to an operational assessment. Spurred by cost growth facing the system, the Office of the Secretary of Defense recently completed a review of the program, subsequently deciding to allow the system to continue development. The Navy is currently executing a reliability growth plan for the system.	2015
Unmanned Surface Vehicle with Unmanned Surface Sweep System	Micro-turbine-powered magnetic towed cable and acoustical signal generator towed from an unmanned surface craft	Prototypes of the unmanned surface vehicle have experienced connectivity and communication issues at distance, reliability issues with their electrical generators, and software malfunctions. Additionally, the Navy is redesigning the cable planned to tow the unmanned surface sweep system due to durability concerns. The unmanned surface sweep system remains in early development.	2015
Rapid Airborne Mine Clearance System	Mounted 30-millimeter gun firing supercavitating projectiles to neutralize near-surface and floating moored mines	Separate engineering development models of the gun and targeting pod have been tested with mixed results. Gun testing demonstrated the need to redesign the bushing (shock absorber). Targeting pod testing revealed problems reacquiring minelike objects and maintaining a gun lock on them. The Navy is rewriting software to address the targeting pod issues.	2017

Source: GAO analysis of Navy data.

For two of the LCS mine countermeasures systems—the Remote Minehunting System and the Airborne Laser Mine Detection System—the Navy has delayed further production pending successful resolution of developmental challenges. These systems both entered production in 2005. According to Navy officials, relaxing the performance requirements for the Remote Minehunting System and the Airborne Laser Mine Detection System is one option under consideration.

- **Airborne Laser Mine Detection System:** Testing of this system has revealed problems detecting mines at the required maximum depth and classifying mines at surface depths. According to Navy officials, the system's required maximum detection depth could be reduced because the system can currently detect mine-like objects at depths that extend below the keels of all ships in the fleet. According to Director, Operational Test and Evaluation officials, however, the system is currently incapable of providing this capability with the required accuracy. Further, Navy officials report that the Remote Minehunting System could provide coverage in near-surface areas of the water that the Airborne Laser Mine Detection System currently cannot reach.

- **Remote Minehunting System:** Operational testing of this system in 2008 revealed significant reliability shortfalls associated with the underwater vehicle. Most notably, the system was only able to function for 7.9 hours before failing—far short of its minimum requirement. Director, Operational Test and Evaluation officials report that since the 2008 event, the Navy's estimated mean time between failures for the system has increased to 45 hours. According to Navy officials, testing and design changes are expected to last into 2011. While the Navy is actively exploring ways to improve Remote Minehunting System reliability, it is also considering reducing the reliability requirement by half.

Surface Warfare

Surface warfare for LCS involves detecting, tracking, and engaging small boat threats; escorting ships; and protecting joint operating areas. Figure 3 illustrates how the surface warfare mission package functions.

Figure 3: Operational Concept for LCS Surface Warfare Systems

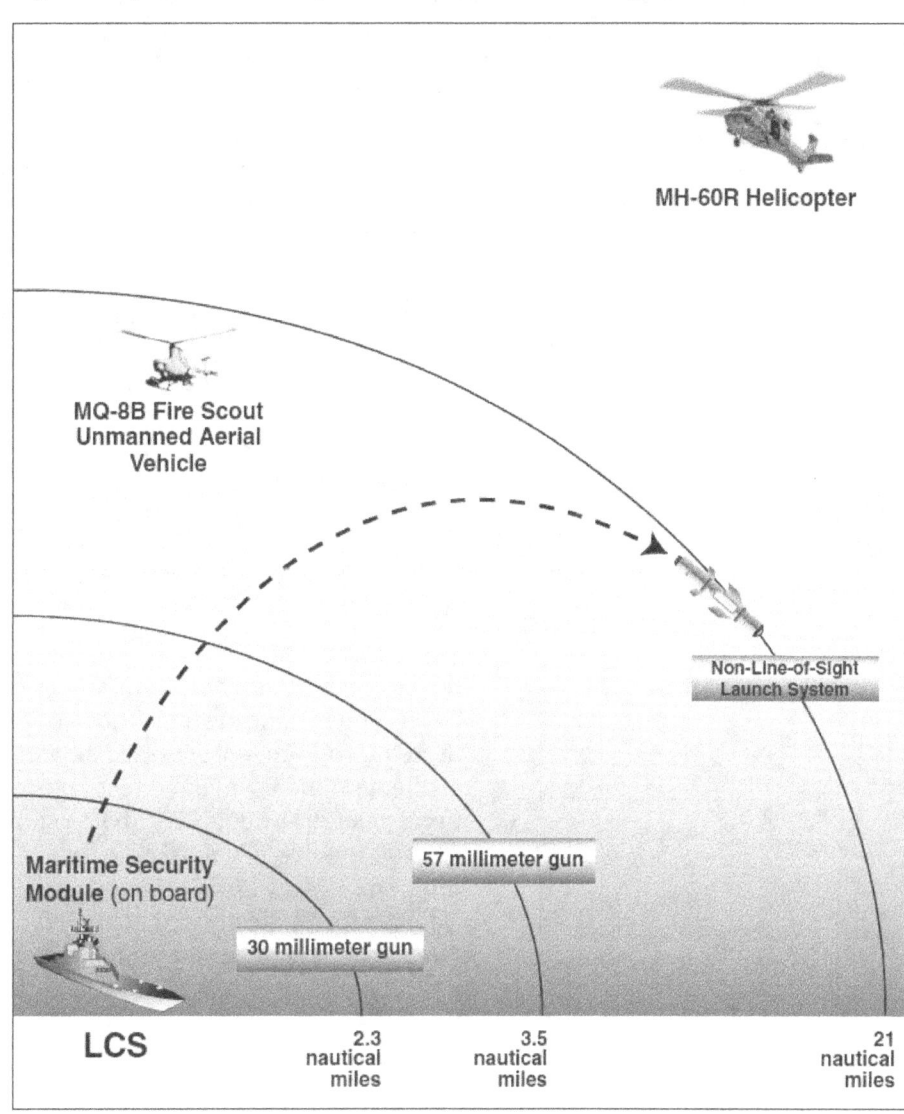

Source: U.S. Navy.

Note: The 57-millimeter gun is a core seaframe system.

Table 5 shows the status of surface warfare mission systems.

Table 5: Navy's Progress Developing and Fielding Surface Warfare Mission Package Systems

Mission system	Capabilities description	Development status	Actual/estimated fielding date
MK 46 30-Millimeter Gun Module	Two-axis stabilized chain gun that can fire up to 250 rounds per minute employing a forward-looking infrared sensor, camera, and laser rangefinder	Structural test firing completed from LCS 1 in September 2009. Currently, the system has not been fully integrated with the combat systems for either of the lead seaframes.	2010
Maritime Security Module	Complement of 19 personnel operating in two teams on LCS that provide capability to conduct visit, board, search, and seizure operations against potential threat vessels	The Navy installed a prototype Maritime Security Module in LCS 1 for the ship's early deployment that included 2 11-meter rigid hull inflatable boats and two berthing/sanitation modules.	2010
Non-Line-of-Sight Launch System	Container launch unit and precision attack missile for use against moving and stationary targets	Testing in July 2009 intended to demonstrate the system's ability to neutralize a target while fired from a rolling platform (similar to a ship) proved unsuccessful due to a malfunctioning sensor and battery connector. During Army operational testing in January and February 2010, the precision attack missile failed to hit its intended target four out of six times. Recent cancellation of the Non-Line-of-Sight Launch System program has prompted the Navy to seek alternatives to include on LCS.	2014

Source: GAO analysis of Navy data.

The surface warfare package remains unproven as a key system, the Non-Line-of-Sight Launch System, was recently canceled prior to completing development. The system—developed under the Army's Future Combat System program—progressed slower than anticipated due to technical challenges and associated test failures. These issues—along with Army fiscal year 2011 budget estimates showing missiles could cost up to $466,000 each—prompted the Army to revisit its commitment to the program. In May 2010, this process culminated with the Under Secretary of Defense for Acquisition, Technology and Logistics approving the Army's request to cancel the program. In response, Navy officials report they are now evaluating potential alternatives to the Non-Line-of-Sight Launch System—including modifications to existing missile systems—to substitute into the surface warfare mission package.

Support Aircraft

In addition to systems outlined above, the Navy plans to employ aircraft in different configurations to execute LCS missions. Table 6 highlights the status of key mission package support aircraft.

Table 6: Navy's Progress Developing and Fielding Key Mission Package Support Aircraft

Mission system	Capabilities description	Development status	Actual/estimated fielding date
MH-60R Helicopter[a]	Ship-based helicopter designed to operate from several types of Navy vessels. Key capabilities include dipping sonar and sonobuoy acoustic sensors, multi-mode radar, electronic warfare sensors, and a forward looking infrared sensor with laser designator. Employs torpedoes, Hellfire air-to-surface missiles, and crew-served mounted machine guns.	Initial operational capability achieved in 2005. September 2009 testing revealed deficiencies associated with the data link (Link 16) and with the automatic video tracking feature of the helicopter's targeting system.	2005
MQ-8B Vertical Take-off and Landing Tactical Unmanned Aerial Vehicle[b]	Unmanned rotary wing air vehicle designed to provide intelligence, surveillance, reconnaissance, and targeting data to tactical users.	Low-rate initial production units are scheduled to complete initial operational test and evaluation onboard a Navy frigate in 2010. The Navy plans to field the system exclusively onboard LCS, where it will connect with and deploy the Coastal Battlefield Reconnaissance and Analysis System. However, integration with the Coastal Battlefield Reconnaissance and Analysis System and LCS seaframes is not scheduled to occur until after the MQ-8B achieves initial operational capability.	2010
MH-60S Helicopter[c]	Helicopter modified into three variants (Fleet Logistics, Airborne Mine Countermeasures, and Armed Helicopter) and optimized for operation in the shipboard/marine environment. Installed systems differ by variant based on mission. The Navy is procuring the Airborne Mine Countermeasures variant in two increments of capability.	Operational testing of the Airborne Mine Countermeasures variant in 2008 was unsuccessful due to reliability issues with the Carriage, Stream, Tow, and Recovery System used to deploy, tow, and retrieve several of the LCS mine countermeasures systems. Further, the on-board command and control console used to monitor and communicate with deployed airborne mine countermeasures systems required a series of software updates to fix computer freezes and other glitches that were degrading performance. The Navy has rescheduled initial operational test and evaluation events for this variant to December 2010.	2011[d]

Source: GAO analysis of Navy data.

[a]MH-60R helicopter supports deployment of the surface warfare and anti-submarine warfare mission packages.

[b]MQ-8B Vertical Take-off and Landing Tactical Unmanned Aerial Vehicle supports deployment of all three LCS mission packages.

[c]MH-60S helicopter supports deployment of the mine countermeasures mission package.

[d]Denotes estimated fielding date for the initial increment of the MH-60S airborne mine countermeasures variant.

In addition to these technical challenges, other factors may constrain availability of the three LCS support aircraft.

- **MH-60R Helicopter:** According to Navy officials, while this system has completed its first deployment with a carrier strike group, the earliest possible date that it will deploy onboard an LCS is the end of fiscal year 2013. Navy officials reported that because of fleet demand for the helicopter, initial MH-60Rs will be assigned to the carrier strike group elements (e.g., destroyers, cruisers, and frigates) before deploying with an LCS. As of January 2010, the Navy had accepted delivery of 46 MH-60Rs of a planned quantity of 252.

- **MH-60S Helicopter:** The Navy has certified flight operations of the armed variant of this helicopter from LCS 1. Previous plans called for only the mine countermeasures variant of the MH-60S to fly from the LCS. As of December 2009, 159 of 275 MH-60S helicopters had been delivered.

- **MQ-8B Vertical Take-off and Landing Tactical Aerial Vehicle (known as Fire Scout):** The Navy is conducting operational testing of Fire Scout onboard a frigate, but intends to field the system with LCS exclusively. Reliability and availability issues uncovered during fiscal year 2010 testing have delayed the program's fielding schedule. Previously, the Navy expected to reach a full-rate production decision on Fire Scout in March 2010. The Navy has since deferred this decision to May 2011.

Developmental Challenges with Individual Systems Have Contributed to Mission Package Procurement Delays

The Navy is buying mission packages through an incremental approach by incorporating systems into the respective mission packages when systems achieve minimum performance requirements. Figure 4 illustrates the effect that recent developmental challenges have had upon mission package procurement plans.

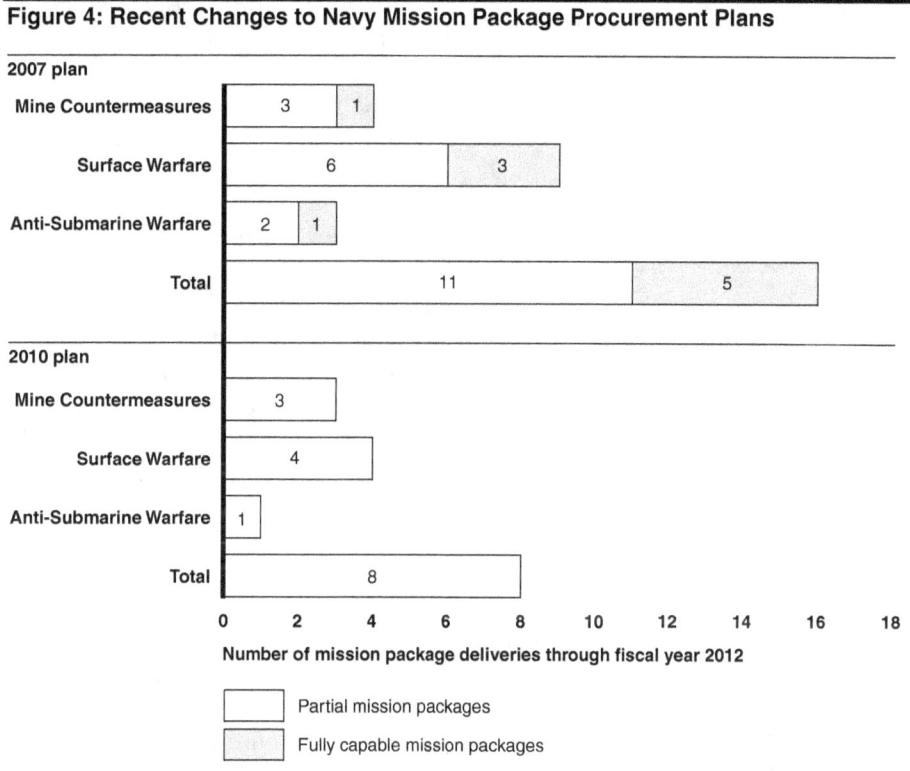

Figure 4: Recent Changes to Navy Mission Package Procurement Plans

Source: GAO analysis of Navy data.

In 2007, the Navy anticipated that a total of 16 mission packages would be delivered by 2012 with all three types of mission packages reaching their full configuration by that date. In recent years, the Navy has deferred planned procurements of LCS mission packages due, in part, to developmental challenges facing mission systems. Under the Navy's 2010 plan, the Navy plans to acquire 8 mission packages by 2012 with no mission package having achieved its full configuration of capabilities.

To date, the Navy has taken delivery of five partial mission packages—two surface warfare, two mine countermeasures, and one anti-submarine warfare. The Navy delayed procurement of the fiscal year 2009 funded mine countermeasures package due to technical issues and resulting operational testing delays. Delivery of the two partial surface warfare mission packages occurred in July 2008 and March 2010, respectively. The first surface warfare package included two engineering development models for the 30-millimeter gun, but did not include the launcher or missiles for the Non-Line-of-Sight Launch System. The second surface warfare mission package included the 30-millimeter gun module and the launcher component—but no missiles—for the Non-Line-of-Sight Launch System.

Because of planned configuration changes to the anti-submarine warfare mission package, the Navy does not plan to buy additional quantities of this package until the new configuration is settled. According to Navy officials, recent warfighting analyses showed that the baseline anti-submarine warfare package did not contribute significantly to the anti-submarine warfare mission. The first package will undergo developmental testing, with results used to inform decisions on future configuration. The Navy conducted end-to-end testing on the first anti-submarine warfare mission package in April 2009 and plans to continue developmental testing in fiscal year 2010. During the 2009 end-to-end test, the Navy found that the unmanned surface vehicle and its associated sensors will require reliability and interface improvements to support sustained undersea warfare.

Mission Package Procurement Delays Could Disrupt Program Plans for Simultaneously Acquiring Seaframes and Mission Packages and Will Limit the Ships' Utility During Initial Deployments

While the Navy now plans to purchase 17 ships and 13 mission packages between fiscal year 2011 and fiscal year 2015, developmental delays facing key mission package systems have positioned the Navy to acquire significant numbers of seaframes before mission packages are proven. This development represents a reversal for the LCS program. In prior years, the Navy deferred purchase of mission packages to account for delays in constructing seaframes. However, as key mission package systems entered operational testing—producing less than successful results—and seaframe design and construction progressed, planned alignment of seaframe and mission package purchases suffered further disruption.

Until mission package performance is proven, the Navy risks investing in a fleet of ships that does not deliver its promised capability. As the Navy stated, the underlying strength of the LCS lies in its innovative design—interchangeable mission equipment that allows the ship to be used for different missions. Fundamental to this approach is the capability to rapidly install interchangeable mission packages into the seaframe. Absent significant capability within its mission packages, seaframe functionality is largely constrained to self-defense as opposed to mission-related tasks.

In addition, the Navy has deployed LCS 1 earlier than originally scheduled and is evaluating a similar course for LCS 2. For these deployments, the Navy is employing hybrid—limited and incomplete—versions of mission packages. The package on LCS 1 includes one mission system (two 30-millimeter guns), the armed variant of the MH-60S helicopter, and the maritime security module. According to Navy officials, deploying LCS 1 two years ahead of schedule allows them to incorporate lessons that can only be learned in a deployment setting. LCS 1 will conduct operations where it will be able to take advantage of its speed and will be equipped with an incomplete version of the surface warfare package. Because the surface warfare mission package is incomplete, the range of missions LCS 1 is capable of executing will be constrained during its initial deployment.

Furthermore, the surface warfare mission package onboard LCS 1 has yet to be fully integrated with the seaframe and lacks key capabilities necessary to defeat surface threats. For example, the 30-millimeter guns have undergone testing with the LCS 1 seaframe, but have yet to be fully integrated with the ship's combat suite. Also, while the guns provide a close range self-defense capability, Navy officials report LCS 1 is currently unable to automatically transfer tracking data from the ship's radar to the 30-millimeter guns. In addition, because of excess MH-60R helicopter demands, the Navy has assigned the armed helo variant of the MH-60S helicopter to LCS 1 for its maiden deployment. Although this MH-60S variant carries air-to-surface missiles and crew-served side machine guns (among other offensive capabilities), it does not have the multi-mode radar found on the MH-60R—a shortfall that could constrain LCS 1's ability to execute surface warfare missions.

Mission Package Delays Coupled with Early Deployment of LCS Seaframes Require Deferral of Key Test Events

Neither LCS seaframe design—nor any of the three LCS mission packages—has completed initial operational test and evaluation. Normally after a lead ship completes its post-delivery maintenance period, initial operational test and evaluation occurs—generally planned for within 1 year of ship delivery. In the case of LCS, initial operational test and evaluation will encompass both seaframes and mission packages. Under the program's 2008 Test and Evaluation Master Plan, LCS 1 was to begin operational testing with the initial systems in the mine countermeasures mission package in the second quarter of fiscal year 2010. The mission systems that were to be tested included the Remote Minehunting System, the MH-60S helicopter (mine countermeasures variant), AN/AQS-20A mine detecting sonar, Unmanned Surface Vehicle with Unmanned Surface Sweep System, Airborne Mine Neutralization System, and Airborne Laser Mine Detection System. However, as noted above, these mission systems have experienced developmental challenges and none are ready to be tested on the seaframe. The Navy has since postponed operational testing of the mine countermeasures mission package to the second quarter of fiscal year 2013, now planned to occur onboard LCS 2.

In addition, early deployments of seaframes postpone their availability to complete planned testing events. For example, although LCS 1 deployed 2 years earlier than scheduled, its first operational testing event with a mission package was delayed by 3 years.[9] The Navy faces several risks in deploying the LCS 1 before it has completed initial operational test and evaluation. For example, Department of Defense testing officials stated that because LCS 1 and LCS 2 are such revolutionary designs, the lead ships should be put through a rigorous testing and evaluation process—in a controlled environment—to best understand their capabilities and limitations. Additionally, the testing officials reported that the ship's maintenance and support strategy was of significant concern to them. According to the testing officials, LCS—more so than other ships—will have to rely heavily on shore-based support, which is an unproven concept.

Incomplete Cost Analyses in the LCS Program Have Undermined Program Progress

The Navy entered contract negotiations in 2009 for fiscal year 2010 funded seaframes with an incomplete understanding of LCS program costs. These contract negotiations proved unsuccessful, prompting the Navy to revise its acquisition strategy for the program. The contractors' proposals for construction of the next three ships exceeded the approximate $1.4 billion in funds the Navy had allocated in its fiscal year 2010 budget. In response, the Navy revised its strategy to construct one seaframe design instead of two for fiscal year 2010 ships and beyond in an effort to improve affordability. Navy cost analyses completed prior to the failed negotiations in 2009 lack several characteristics essential to a high quality cost estimate. These characteristics include the completion of sensitivity and uncertainty analyses and an independent review of the cost estimate. The

---

[9]Under the LCS program's 2008 Test and Evaluation Master Plan, the Navy planned to conduct an operational assessment of LCS 1—employing elements of the first mine countermeasures mission package—beginning the second quarter of fiscal year 2010. The Navy's fiscal year 2011 budget estimates show LCS 1 will now begin operational testing in the third quarter of fiscal year 2013 using the surface warfare mission package.

Navy plans to complete a more comprehensive cost estimate before award of additional ship contracts in 2010.

Unsuccessful Contract Negotiations in Late 2009 Prompted the Navy to Restructure Its Acquisition Strategy for the LCS Program

The Navy budgeted $1.38 billion in fiscal year 2010 for construction of three ships (LCS 5, LCS 6, and LCS 7) at a cost of $460 million each. The Navy planned to award construction contracts for these ships in November 2009, to include the purchase of at least one ship of each LCS seaframe design. Navy officials were confident they had gained sufficient knowledge from construction activities associated with the first four seaframes to support a cost efficient, dual design strategy going forward. As part of this strategy, the Navy solicited proposals from each of the LCS prime contractors for construction of up to three ships on a fixed-price basis. The industry teams returned their proposals in August 2009 and, according to Navy officials, included pricing significantly above the Navy's expectations. Lockheed Martin and General Dynamics officials stated that the fixed-price terms the Navy sought prompted a forthright assessment of remaining program risks—including technical, design, and funding uncertainties—and subsequent pricing of that risk in their proposals.

Due to the sharp differences between the Navy cost expectations and the contractor proposals with respect to LCS pricing, the Navy concluded the negotiations without awarding contracts for any new ships. Further, Navy leadership stated it had no reasonable basis to find that the LCS program would be executable going forward under the current acquisition strategy, which prompted the Navy to outline a new acquisition strategy in September 2009 aimed at improving program affordability by selecting one design for the fiscal year 2010 ships and beyond. Under the terms of the new strategy, the Navy will contract with a single source on a fixed-price basis for up to 10 ships (2 ships awarded per year) through fiscal year 2014. The strategy also outlines plans to issue a second solicitation for up to another 5 ships to be constructed at a separate yard with awards planned between fiscal years 2012 and 2014. The first source will provide the combat systems for the 5 additional ships constructed by the second shipyard. Navy officials stated that the new acquisition approach will produce cost benefits attributable to near-term competitive pricing pressures between the two current LCS shipbuilding teams, economic order quantity purchases of key materials, efficiencies associated with potentially moving to a single, common combat system, and significantly reduced total ownership costs for the Navy.

While the new acquisition strategy for the LCS program promises improved affordability, the Navy's failure to recognize the unexecutable nature of the previous strategy—before engaging in the costly, time consuming process of requesting proposals—has not come without penalty. Contract awards for LCS 5, LCS 6, and LCS 7 have been delayed by at least 9 months, subsequently disrupting planned workloads—and potentially increasing the overhead costs charged to existing Navy contracts—in the LCS shipyards. Most importantly, however, the unsuccessful negotiations and revised strategy represent the latest delay to delivery of promised capabilities to the fleet, which is depending heavily on LCS to take over several current and future missions. Figure 5 highlights the resequencing of key LCS program events following the revised acquisition strategy, which delayed contract awards for the fiscal year 2010 funded ships.

Figure 5: Schedule of Key Near-term Events as Outlined in the LCS Program's 2009 and 2010 Acquisition Strategies

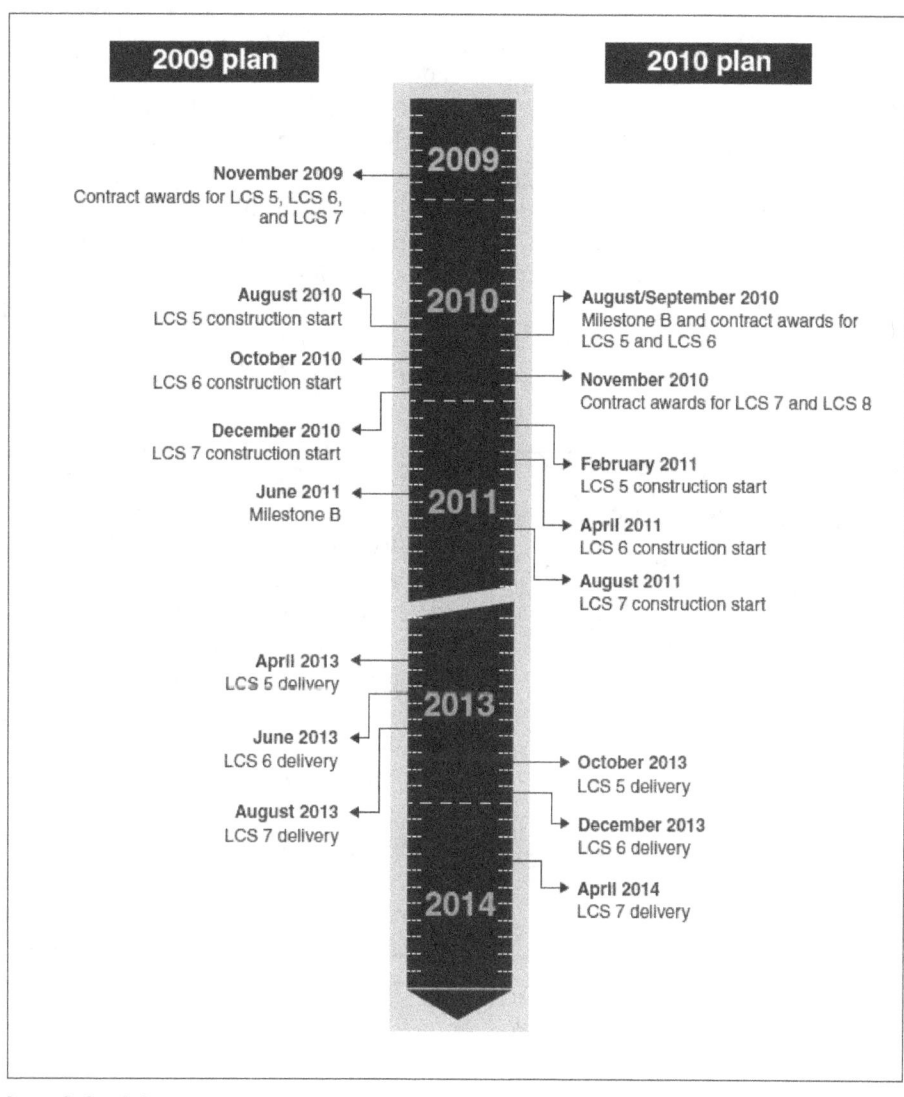

Source: GAO analysis.

Under the new acquisition strategy, the LCS program must complete a major program review (milestone B) before award of fiscal year 2010 ship contracts. The previous acquisition strategy deferred this review until June 2011—after award of the three fiscal year 2010 ship contracts. While holding the milestone B decision earlier than planned is an improvement, most ship programs align milestone B with the decision to authorize the

GAO-10-523 Littoral Combat Ship

start of detail design—a decision that dates back to 2004 in the LCS program.

In support of the milestone B review, Department of Defense policy requires the Navy to provide its own cost estimate for the program.[10] In response, the Navy plans to submit a program life cycle cost estimate, which will be completed by Naval Sea Systems Command's Cost Engineering and Industrial Analysis division. In addition, federal statute requires that for major defense acquisition programs (including LCS), an independent estimate of life cycle costs be prepared and provided to the milestone decision authority before the approval is given to proceed with Engineering and Manufacturing Development.[11] The responsibility for the independent cost estimate is assigned to the Director, Cost Assessment and Program Evaluation within the Department of Defense.

Navy Cost Analyses Completed Ahead of Contract Negotiations in 2009 Lacked Key Elements Needed to Ensure High Quality

Because the Department of Defense has not yet completed a milestone B review of the LCS program—to include development and evaluation of a comprehensive Navy cost estimate and independent cost estimate—the typical mechanisms and processes for assessing program affordability were not carried out ahead of the Navy's 2009 contract negotiations, which turned out to be unsuccessful. Instead, Navy officials reported their cost expectations for fiscal year 2010 funded seaframes were largely framed by the pricing agreements reached with Lockheed Martin and General Dynamics for LCS 3 and LCS 4 construction, respectively. Apart from this data, the Navy had few alternative sources available that forecast LCS program costs. Most prominent of these sources was analysis completed in June 2009 as part of the LCS total ownership cost baseline estimate.[12] The Navy chartered this estimate to investigate ways it could alter the LCS seaframe designs to reduce its total ownership cost in the program. The estimate reflected the life cycle costs of the proposed two-design, 55 ship LCS class—not including mission packages—and was divided into

---

[10]Department of Defense Instruction 5000.02, *Operation of the Defense Acquisition System* Enclosure 4 Table 3 (Dec. 8, 2008).

[11]Engineering and manufacturing development has the same meaning as system development and demonstration as referred to in 10 U.S.C. § 2434.

[12]In June 2009, Navy cost estimators completed their preliminary analysis of LCS total ownership costs and briefed key findings to senior Navy leaders. The Navy later recorded this analysis in the *LCS Total Ownership Cost Baseline Estimate Documentation* (Aug. 25, 2009).

sections covering (1) research, development, testing, and evaluation; (2) procurement; and (3) operations and support costs. The estimate also updated a set of previous Navy and Department of Defense estimates for LCS 3 and LCS 4 that were completed in November 2008 in support of the program's milestone A-Prime review[13] and March and May 2009 contract awards for those ships.

Our analysis of the procurement section of the LCS total ownership cost baseline found the estimate lacks several characteristics essential to a high-quality cost estimate.[14] To complete this analysis, we compared the Navy's estimate to best practices criteria, as outlined in GAO's Cost Estimating and Assessment Guide and presented in appendix II.[15] These criteria characterize high-quality cost estimates as those that are credible, comprehensive, well-documented, and accurate. Table 7 highlights the key findings of our analysis.

---

[13]On December 18, 2008, the Defense Acquisition Board conducted a Milestone A-Prime review of the LCS program to determine the readiness of the program to continue the Technology Development phase and to procure fiscal year 2009 ships and mission packages.

[14]We previously assessed the quality of the Navy's operating and support cost estimates for LCS. See GAO, *Littoral Combat Ship: Actions Needed to Improve Operating Cost Estimates and Mitigate Risks in Implementing New Concepts*, GAO-10-257 (Washington, D.C.: Feb. 2, 2010).

[15]See GAO, *GAO Cost Estimating and Assessment Guide: Best Practices for Developing and Managing Capital Program Costs*, GAO-09-3SP (Washington, D.C.: Mar. 2009).

Table 7: Extent to Which the Navy's Total Ownership Cost Baseline Estimate for LCS Procurement Was Well-Documented, Comprehensive, Accurate, and Credible

Four characteristics of high-quality cost estimates and 12 key steps[a]	Not met	Minimally met	Partially met	Mostly met	Fully met
Well-documented			X		
Define the estimate's purpose (Step 1)				X	
Define the program characteristics (Step 3)			X		
Identify ground rules and assumptions (Step 5)		X			
Obtain the data (Step 6)				X	
Document the estimate (Step 10)		X			
Present the estimate to management for approval (Step 11)			X		
Comprehensive			X		
Develop the estimating plan (Step 2)			X		
Determine the estimating approach (Step 4)				X	
Identify ground rules and assumptions (Step 5)		X			
Accurate			X		
Develop the point estimate and compare to an independent cost estimate (Step 7)			X		
Update the estimate to reflect actual costs and changes (Step 12)				X	
Credible		X			
Develop the point estimate and compare to an independent cost estimate (Step 7)			X		
Conduct a sensitivity analysis (Step 8)		X			
Conduct risk and uncertainty analysis (Step 9)	X				

Source: GAO analysis of Navy data.

[a]These 12 steps are outlined in additional detail in appendix II.

Note: The ratings used in this analysis are as follows: "Not met" means that the Navy did not provide evidence that satisfied the criterion; "Minimally met" means that the Navy provided evidence that satisfies a small portion of the criterion; "Partially met" means that the Navy provided evidence that satisfies about half of the criterion; "Mostly met" means that the Navy provided evidence that satisfies a large portion of the criterion; "Fully met" means that the Navy provided complete evidence that satisfies the entire criterion.

In developing the LCS total ownership cost baseline estimate, the Navy excluded certain key costs, used overly optimistic assumptions, inadequately documented its analyses, and did not perform analyses needed to identify levels of confidence and certainty in the cost estimate. As a result of these weaknesses, the LCS program total ownership cost baseline estimate is not reliable for decision making.

| Well-documented | Cost estimates are *well-documented* when they can be easily repeated or updated and can be traced to original sources through auditing. Rigorous documentation increases the credibility of an estimate and helps support an organization's decision making process. The documentation should explicitly identify the primary methods, calculations, results, rationales, assumptions, and sources of the data used to generate each cost element. All the steps involved in developing the estimate should be documented so that a cost analyst unfamiliar with the program can recreate the estimate with the same result. |

The level of documentation detailing the Navy's LCS procurement cost model is insufficient for someone unfamiliar with the program to easily recreate the estimate. The level of detail in the total ownership cost estimate does not reflect the full level of detail available for the LCS program, leaving managers with incomplete information on which to base program decisions. The Navy documented the LCS technical baseline in a July 2006 report—the Cost Analysis Requirements Description— describing program requirements, purpose, technical characteristics, development plan, acquisition strategy, operational plan, and risks. Navy estimators, however, did not rely upon this document in developing their estimate because the Cost Analysis Requirements Document is out of date and does not reflect current program approaches, seaframe configurations, and developmental challenges. Alternatively, Navy cost estimators relied on the current LCS build specification, ship weight reports, and known design changes to inform their understanding of the ships' technical characteristics. Since then, the Navy reports it has updated the LCS Cost Analysis Requirements Document in anticipation of the program's milestone B review.

In addition, the Navy divided the procurement content of its estimate into cost categories for plans, basic construction, change orders, government furnished equipment, other items, and outfitting and post-delivery. For most of these elements, Navy cost estimators relied on historical data and subject matter experts as sources of data. For the basic construction cost element, the Navy relied primarily on contractor cost proposals dating to May 2008 and November 2008. According to the Navy, the proposal data provided an accurate starting point for basic construction cost modeling because industry teams were instructed to base their proposals on their actual labor and material costs and/or estimates for lead ships. The Navy reports it traced the proposal data to November 2008 cost performance reports submitted by the contractors. The Navy then adjusted the proposals' estimates for labor hours and materials to reflect, for instance, known changes in pricing.

However, as we recently reported, earned value management systems in each of the LCS shipyards do not meet Defense Contract Management Agency requirements for validation.[16] Consequently, cost and schedule data reported by the prime contractors cannot be considered fully reliable.[17] The LCS cost estimate does not include any evidence that the Navy adjusted its basic construction cost estimates to account for this uncertainty.

Comprehensive

Estimates are *comprehensive* when they contain a level of detail that ensures that all pertinent costs are included and no costs are double-counted. It is important to ensure the completeness, consistency, and realism of the information contained in the cost estimate.

The Navy chartered a working group at the outset of the total ownership cost baseline estimate. Group members included representatives from the Naval Center for Cost Analysis; Naval Sea Systems Command's Ship Engineering and Logistics, Maintenance, and Industrial Operations directorates; Chief of Naval Operations' Surface Warfare directorate, Space and Naval Warfare Systems Command; Program Executive Office for Integrated Warfare Systems; and the RAND Corporation. This group developed a study plan for the LCS estimate that identified goals, set deadlines for completing key tasks, and outlined required resources. In addition, the group met biweekly and provided cross-checks and verification to the Navy cost team's estimating assumptions and results. Upon completion of the procurement cost analysis, Navy estimators briefed out results to the Commander, Naval Sea Systems Command, in June 2009.

Further, our analysis found that the Navy's LCS estimate identifies ground rules and assumptions from which the estimate is derived. However, it does not identify potential effects that changes to key assumptions—such as allocation of ships between contractors and changes to the technical baseline of the ship—could have upon the cost estimate. Also, the estimate does not identify how budget constraints could affect program plans or the potential effects that continued design refinements to the lead ships may have upon construction cost outcomes of follow-on ships.

---

[16]See GAO, *Defense Acquisitions: Assessments of Selected Weapons Programs*, GAO-10-388SP (Washington, D.C.: Mar. 30, 2010).

[17]Under the terms of the LCS 3 and LCS 4 contracts, the shipyards must achieve earned value management system certification within 28 months from the date of contract award.

In addition, the Navy did not complete evaluations of risk distributions for its cost estimating assumptions. Alternatively, cost estimators relied on discussions with ship designers, engineers, and technicians from the Navy and contractors to identify the scope of certain procurement cost elements. Navy cost analysts report they will complete evaluations of risk distributions for assumptions used in the LCS program life cycle cost estimate being developed for the milestone B review.

The Navy also relied upon industry-provided work breakdown structures for LCS 1, LCS 2, and LCS 3—that it then mapped to its own ship work breakdown structure—to identify the work tasks necessary to deliver LCS seaframes. Following completion of the total ownership cost estimate, the Navy received the LCS 4 work breakdown structure from industry, which it will use in developing the milestone B program life cycle cost estimate.

Accurate

Estimates are *accurate* when they are based on an assessment of the costs most likely to be incurred. Therefore, when costs change, best practices require that the estimate be updated to reflect changes in technical or program assumptions and new phases or milestones.

The total ownership cost baseline estimate discretely estimated LCS 3 and LCS 4 basic construction costs separate from the cost performance outcomes being realized on LCS 1 and LCS 2. This approach was used because, according to Navy cost estimators, distinguishing nonrecurring work on the first two ships from work that would recur on future ships—a necessary step for deriving follow-on ship costs—was too challenging an undertaking given the major design changes and construction rework that occurred on the lead ships. Further, LCS 3 and LCS 4 represented a slightly different technical baseline from LCS 1 and LCS 2, leading the Navy to judge it more appropriate to use the initial follow-on ships as the basis of estimates for future ships.

After developing their cost estimates for LCS 3 and LCS 4, the Navy estimators applied a 94 percent learning curve to the basic construction cost elements to arrive at construction estimates for future ships of each design. However, because Austal USA and Marinette Marine have only recently begun building complex Navy ships such as LCS, the historical data available to Navy cost analysts for deriving an accurate learning curve was constrained. As a result, the Navy developed its LCS learning curve based primarily on construction outcomes for alternative vessels and, in some cases, alternative shipyards including (1) 14 Coast Guard buoy tenders built at Marinette Marine, (2) 13 Cyclone-class coastal patrol ships built at Bollinger Shipyards, and (3) 10 patrol craft built at Austal facilities in Australia. According to the Navy, this data produced a widely varied range of potential LCS learning curves, which contributed to the Navy's decision to arrive at a curve for LCS that was toward the high end of the range (i.e., more conservative).

Navy cost estimators stated that their current work to develop a program life cycle cost estimate for LCS precludes future updates to the total ownership cost baseline. Additional cost estimates post-milestone B in the program will rely on the program life cycle cost estimate—and corresponding independent cost analysis—as starting points.

Credible

Estimates are *credible* when they have been cross-checked with an independent cost estimate and when a level of uncertainty associated with the estimate has been identified. An independent cost estimate provides the estimator with an unbiased test of the reasonableness of the estimate and reduces the cost risk associated with the project by demonstrating that alternative methods generate similar results.

Our analysis found that the total ownership cost baseline was not compared to an independent cost estimate. Comparing against an independent cost estimate provides an unbiased test of whether a program office or service-level cost estimate is reasonable. It is also used to identify risks related to budget shortfalls or excesses. According to Navy officials, the total ownership cost estimate was not tied to a major program milestone. As such, development of a corresponding independent cost estimate was not required. The Navy did, however, complete peer reviews, engage in discussions with program officials for classes of ships used as analogies in the estimate, and utilize expert opinion and work groups to cross-check for accuracy and omissions.

In addition, we found the Navy did not complete sensitivity or uncertainty analyses for LCS procurement cost elements. A sensitivity analysis provides a range of costs that span a best and worst case spread. In general, it is better for decision makers to know the range of potential costs that surround a point estimate and the reasons behind what drives that range than to just have a point estimate from which to make decisions. Sensitivity analysis can provide a clear picture of both the high and low costs that can be expected, with discrete reasons for what drives them. Uncertainty analysis provides the basis for adjusting estimates to reflect unknown facts and circumstances that could affect costs, and it identifies risk associated with the cost estimate. In order to inform decision makers about the likelihood of success, an uncertainty analysis should be performed for every cost estimate, as an organization varies the effects of multiple elements on costs, and as a result, can express a level of confidence in the point estimate. Further, because numerous risks can influence the estimate, they should be examined for their sources of uncertainty and potential effect, and they should be modeled to determine how they can affect the uncertainty of the cost estimate.

Navy cost estimators identified major procurement cost drivers in the program, but do not plan to complete sensitivity or uncertainty analyses for those drivers until shortly before milestone B. Navy officials cited the change to the program's acquisition strategy shortly following completion of the total ownership cost estimate as their rationale for deferring these analyses. Without sensitivity and uncertainty analyses, the Navy cannot fully account for the effect various risks can have on the overall total ownership cost estimate.

Conclusions

The Navy is counting on LCS as its primary means to defeat sea mines, counter low-end surface threats, and prosecute enemy submarines in coastal waters. Further, LCS—with its planned 55 seaframes and 64 mission packages—represents a large component of the Navy's future surface fleet, making it key to the Navy's ability to maintain global presence.

However, the Navy's ability to deliver a capable, affordable LCS remains unproven. Staying within budget will require the Navy to achieve design stability before beginning construction of future ships. Moreover, LCS testing remains in its infancy, as the first operational testing event involving a seaframe and partial mission package has been deferred to fiscal year 2013. In addition, the Navy now expects individual mission package systems to remain in development through 2017. Until LCS capabilities are demonstrated through operational testing, the Navy cannot be certain that the seaframes and mission packages it is buying will be able to execute the missions that the fleet plans to assign to LCS vessels.

Further, decisions to deploy the lead ship early and complete previously unplanned maintenance periods have rendered current program test plans obsolete. Testing delays to key mission package elements—followed by prudent Navy decisions to defer new procurements of these systems— have created an imbalance between seaframe and mission package acquisition plans. For example, the Navy now plans to fund construction of 17 seaframes between fiscal years 2011 and 2015—whereas only 13 mission packages will be purchased during that time. This situation could be exacerbated should the Navy encounter additional difficulties resolving the substantial technical issues facing the mine countermeasures package.

In addition, although the Navy has emphasized the importance of affordability to successful outcomes in the LCS program, it continues to make key investment decisions without a clear understanding of program costs. For LCS, the Navy determined it appropriate to award contracts for four ships and conduct negotiations for three more without completing a detailed, programwide, independent cost estimate—a strategy that contributed to less than optimal results. High-quality cost estimates are well-documented, comprehensive, accurate, and credible—characteristics that are not fully embodied in the Navy's most recent cost estimate for LCS procurement. Shortfalls include the lack of sensitivity and uncertainty analyses and an independent review of the cost estimate. Continuing technical challenges and design changes on initial seaframes further complicate the Navy's efforts to identify future LCS costs. Until these issues are resolved, and a high-quality estimate of program costs is developed, the Navy cannot be confident that the LCS capabilities it promises can be attained at prices it is willing to pay.

Recommendations for Executive Action

We recommend the Secretary of Defense take the following four actions:

To attain the level of knowledge needed to retire design risk and reduce construction disruptions, ensure changes identified in building and testing the first four ships are incorporated into the basic and functional design by the start of construction for future LCS seaframes.

To provide a meaningful framework for evaluating seaframe and mission package performance, update the LCS test and evaluation master plan to (1) account for any early deployments of seaframes and the significant developmental challenges faced by key mission package systems and (2) identify alternative approaches for completing seaframe and mission package initial operational test and evaluation.

To safeguard against excess quantities of ships and mission packages being purchased before their combined capabilities are demonstrated, update the LCS acquisition strategy to account for operational testing delays in the program and resequence planned purchases of ships and mission packages, as appropriate.

To provide a sound basis for future LCS investment decisions, ensure that future LCS cost estimates—including the program life cycle cost estimate currently planned for milestone B—are well-documented, comprehensive, accurate, and credible.

Agency Comments and Our Evaluation

The Department of Defense agreed with all of our recommendations. However, in responding to our recommendation to ensure changes identified in building and testing the first four ships are incorporated into the basic and functional design by the start of construction for future LCS seaframes, the department stated that the program can use existing ship and class design services contracts to execute additional changes after contract award. As our prior work has shown, however, this practice has been tried before in Navy shipbuilding programs and has consistently contributed to ship deliveries that are over cost and behind schedule. As such, we would expect the Navy to set the bar extremely high for making design changes to ships that are already under construction.

The department's written comments can be found in appendix III of this report. The department also provided technical comments, which were incorporated into the report as appropriate.

We are sending copies of this report to interested congressional committees, the Secretary of Defense, and the Secretary of the Navy. The report is also available at no charge on the GAO Web site at http://www.gao.gov.

If you or your staff have any questions about this report, please contact me at (202) 512-4841 or martinb@gao.gov. Contact points for our Offices of Congressional Relations and Public Affairs may be found on the last page of this report. GAO staff who made major contributions to this report are listed in appendix IV.

Belva M. Martin
Acting Director
Acquisition and Sourcing Management

Appendix I: Scope and Methodology

This report evaluates Littoral Combat Ship (LCS) planning and implementation efforts. Specifically, we (1) identified technical, design, and construction challenges to completing the first four seaframes within current cost and schedule estimates, (2) assessed the Navy's progress developing and fielding mission packages, and (3) evaluated the quality of recent Navy cost analyses for seaframes and their effect on program progress.

To identify challenges in completing the first four seaframes, we analyzed Department of Defense and contractor-generated documents that addressed technical challenges and cost and schedule performance for LCS seaframes including Navy test reports; Navy Supervisor of Shipbuilding reports; monthly contract performance reports; integrated baseline reviews; reports to Congress; sea trial reports for the first two ships; and construction progress briefings. To identify design changes and to understand the impact of these changes to the construction processes for seaframes, we reviewed LCS contracts and change orders; program schedules for LCS 3 and LCS 4; monthly contract performance reports; weekly Supervisor of Shipbuilding reports; and quarterly ship production progress conference briefings. We also reviewed information from contractors outlining process improvements and capital investments at each of the LCS shipyards aimed at increasing capability and capacity needed to support efficient construction of LCS seaframes. To further corroborate documentary evidence and gather additional information in support of our review, we conducted interviews with relevant Navy and industry officials responsible for managing the design and construction of LCS seaframes, such as the LCS Seaframe program office; Program Executive Office, Ships; Supervisor of Shipbuilding officials; Lockheed Martin and General Dynamics (LCS prime contractors); Marinette Marine and Austal USA (LCS shipbuilders); and MTU (LCS 2 and LCS 4 diesel engine vendor). We also held discussions with LCS technical authorities, testing agents, and requirements officers from Naval Sea Systems Command's Ship Engineering directorate; Director, Operational Test and Evaluation; American Bureau of Shipping; Commander, Navy Operational Test and Evaluation Force; Office of the Chief of Naval Operations' Surface Warfare directorate; and Naval Surface Warfare Center-Panama City division.

To assess the Navy's progress developing and fielding mission packages, we analyzed documents outlining LCS mission package development plans and performance including program schedules, test reports, and budget submissions. In order to evaluate the realism of mission package testing and procurement plans, we analyzed and compared mission package development schedules and test reports against LCS seaframe construction, delivery, and testing schedules. To further corroborate documentary evidence and gather additional information in support of our review, we held discussions with Navy program offices and Department of Defense agencies responsible for acquiring and testing key LCS mission systems including the Program Executive Office for Littoral and Mine Warfare; LCS Mission Modules program office; Unmanned Maritime Vehicles program office; and the Mine Warfare program office; Director, Operational Test and Evaluation; Commander, Operational Test and Evaluation Force, Navy. To gather additional information on remaining risks to mission package development and integration, we interviewed relevant Navy officials from the MH-60R Helicopter program office, MH-60S Helicopter program office, Navy and Marine Corps Tactical Multi-Mission Unmanned Aerial Systems program office, and Naval Surface Warfare Center-Panama City division.

To evaluate the quality of recent Navy cost analyses for LCS seaframes, we compared the Navy's total ownership cost baseline estimate for LCS procurement to best practices criteria as outlined in GAO's Cost Estimating and Assessment Guide. These criteria characterize high-quality cost estimates as those that are credible, comprehensive, well-documented, and accurate. To supplement our analysis and gain additional visibility into the Navy's process for developing its LCS estimate, we interviewed officials from Naval Sea Systems Command's Cost Engineering and Analysis directorate; LCS Seaframe program officials; and the Director, Cost Assessment and Program Evaluation.

We conducted this performance audit from July 2009 to August 2010 in accordance with generally accepted government auditing standards. Those standards require that we plan and perform the audit to obtain sufficient, appropriate evidence to provide a reasonable basis for our findings and conclusions based on our audit objectives. We believe that the evidence obtained provides a reasonable basis for our findings and conclusions based on our audit objectives.

Appendix II: GAO Methodology Used to Perform Cost Estimating Analysis

To evaluate estimated Littoral Combat Ship (LCS) seaframe procurement costs as outlined in the Navy's total ownership cost baseline (August 2009), GAO employed criteria from our Cost Estimating and Assessment Guide.[1] In developing this guide, GAO cost experts identified 12 steps consistently applied by cost-estimating organizations throughout the federal government and industry and considered best practices for the development of reliable cost estimates. These 12 steps—and their related measures—are identified below.

Step One: Define the Estimate's Purpose
- Are the purpose and scope of the cost estimate defined and documented?
    a. Is the level of detail the estimate is conducted at consistent with the level of detail available for the program?
    b. Have all applicable costs been estimated, including life cycle costs?
    c. Is the scope of the estimate defined and documented?

Step Two: Develop the Estimating Plan
- Did the team develop a written study plan that:
    a. Determined the estimating team's composition and whether the team is from a centralized office;
    b. Identified which subject matter experts the team will rely on for information;
    c. Outlined the estimating approach (see Step four);
    d. Identified a master schedule for completing the estimate that provided adequate time to do the work.

Step Three: Define the Program Characteristics
- Is there a documented technical baseline description that is contained in a single document? If yes, does it include the following:
    a. What the program is supposed to do—requirements;
    b. How the program will fulfill its mission—purpose;
    c. What it will look like—technical characteristics;
    d. Where and how the program will be built—development plan;
    e. How the program will be acquired—acquisition strategy;
    f. How the program will operate—operational plan;
    g. Which characteristics affect cost the most—risk.

---

[1] See GAO, *GAO Cost Estimating and Assessment Guide: Best Practices for Developing and Managing Capital Program Costs*, GAO-09-3SP (Washington, D.C.: Mar. 2009).

Step Four: Determine the Estimating Structure
- Is there a defined work breakdown structure (WBS) and/or cost element structure?
    a. Is the WBS product-oriented, traceable to the statement of work, and at an appropriate level of detail to ensure that cost elements are neither omitted nor double-counted?
    b. Is the WBS standardized so that cost data can be collected and used for estimating future programs?
    c. Does the cost estimate WBS match the schedule and earned value management (EVM) WBS?
    d. Is the WBS updated as the program becomes better defined and to reflect changes as they occur?
    e. Is there a WBS dictionary that defines what is included in each element and how it relates to others in the hierarchy?

Step Five: Identify Ground Rules and Assumptions
- Are there defined ground rules and assumptions that document the rationale and any historical data to back up any claims?
    a. Have risks associated with any assumptions been identified and traced to specific WBS elements?
    b. Have budget constraints, as well as the effect of delaying program content, been defined?
    c. Have inflation indices and their source been identified?
    d. If the program depends on a participating agency or agency's equipment have the effects of these assumptions not holding been identified?
    e. Have items excluded from the estimate been documented and explained?
    f. If technology maturity has been assumed, does the estimate address the effect of the assumption's failure on cost and schedule?
    g. Did cost estimators meet with technical staff to determine risk distributions for all assumptions so they could use this information for sensitivity and uncertainty analysis?

Step Six: Obtain the Data
- Was the data gathered from valid historical actual cost, schedule, and program and technical sources?
    a. Do the data apply to the program being estimated and have they been analyzed for cost drivers?
    b. Have the data been collected from primary sources and adequately documented as to the source, content, time, units, an assessment of the accuracy of the data and reliability, and any circumstances affecting the data?

   c. Are data continually collected and stored for future use?
   d. Did analysts meet with the data sources to better understand the program and ask them about the data?
   e. Were the data reviewed and benchmarked against historical data for reasonableness?
   f. Were the data analyzed using scatterplots and descriptive statistics and were they normalized to account for cost, sizing units, etc. so they are consistent for comparisons?

Step Seven: Develop the Point Estimate and Compare It to an Independent Cost Estimate
- Did the cost estimator consider various cost estimating methods like analogy, engineering build up, parametric, extrapolating from actual costs, and expert opinion (if none of the other methods can be used)?
   a. If the parametric method was used as the estimating method, were the cost estimating relationships (CER) statistics examined to determine its quality?
   b. Were learning curves used if there was much manual labor associated with production and were production rate and breaks in production considered?
   c. Was the point estimate developed by aggregating the WBS cost estimates by one of the cost estimating methods?
   d. Were results checked for accuracy, double-counting, and omissions and were validated with cross checks and independent cost estimates?
   e. If software is a major component of the cost estimate were software estimating best practices from Chapter 12 of the Guide addressed?

Step Eight: Conduct a Sensitivity Analysis
- Did the cost estimate include a sensitivity analysis that, using a range of possible costs, identified the effects of changing key cost driver assumptions or factors? Were the following steps taken:
   a. Key cost drivers were identified;
   b. Cost elements representing the highest percentage of cost were determined and their parameters and assumptions were examined;
   c. The total cost was reestimated by varying each parameter between its minimum and maximum range;
   d. Results were documented and the reestimate repeated for each parameter that was a key cost driver;
   e. Outcomes were evaluated for parameters most sensitive to change.

Step Nine: Conduct Risk and Uncertainty Analysis
- Was a risk and uncertainty analysis conducted that quantified the imperfectly understood risks and identified the effects of changing key cost driver assumptions and factors? Were the following steps performed:
  a. A probability distribution was modeled for each cost element's uncertainty based on data availability, reliability, and variability;
  b. The correlation (i.e., relationship) between cost elements was accounted for to capture risk;
  c. A Monte Carlo simulation model was used to develop a distribution of total possible costs and an S curve showing alternative cost estimate probabilities;
  d. The probability associated with the point estimate was identified.
  e. Contingency reserves were recommended for achieving the desired confidence level;
  f. The risk-adjusted cost estimate was allocated, phased, and converted to then year dollars for budgeting, and high-risk elements were identified to mitigate risks;
  g. A risk management plan was implemented jointly with the contractor to identify and analyze risk, plan for risk mitigation, and continually track risk.

Step Ten: Document the Estimate
- Did the documentation describe the cost estimating process, data sources, and methods step by step so that a cost analyst unfamiliar with the program could understand what was done and replicate it?
  a. Are supporting data adequate for easily updating the estimate to reflect actual costs or program changes and using them for future estimates?
  b. Did the documentation describe the estimate with narrative and cost tables and did it contain an executive summary, introduction, and descriptions of methods, with data broken out by WBS cost elements, sensitivity analysis, risk and uncertainty analysis, management approval, and updates that reflect actual costs and changes?
  c. Did the detail address best practices and the 12 steps of high-quality estimates?
  d. Was the documentation mathematically sensible and logical?
  e. Did it discuss contingency reserves and how they were derived from risk and uncertainty analysis?
  f. Did the documentation include access to an electronic copy of the cost model and are both the documentation and the cost model stored so that authorized personnel can easily find and use them for other cost estimates?

Step Eleven: Present the Estimate to Management for Approval
- Was there a briefing to management that included a clear explanation of the cost estimate so as to convey its level of competence?
  a. Did the briefing illustrate the largest cost drivers by presenting them logically with backup charts for responding to more probing questions?
  b. Did the briefing include an overview of the program's technical foundation and objectives, the life cycle cost estimate in time-phased constant year dollars, a discussion of ground rules and assumptions, the method and process for each WBS cost element estimate including data sources, the results of sensitivity and risk/uncertainty analysis along with a confidence interval, the comparison of the point estimate to an independent cost estimate with a discussion of any differences and whether the point estimate is reasonable, an affordability analysis based on funding and contingency reserves, a discussion of any concerns or challenges, conclusions, and recommendations for approval?
  c. Was any feedback from the briefing including management's acceptance of the estimate acted on and recorded in the cost estimate documentation?

Step Twelve: Update the Estimate to Reflect Actual Costs and Changes
- Is there a process for the estimating team to update the estimate with actual costs as it becomes available?
  a. Was the estimate updated to reflect changes in technical or program assumptions and was there a discussion how these changes affected the cost estimate?
  b. Did the cost estimates get replaced with actual costs? Were the actual costs from an EVM system?
  c. Did the estimate discuss lessons learned for elements whose actual costs or schedules differed from the estimate?

Appendix III: Comments from the Department of Defense

OFFICE OF THE UNDER SECRETARY OF DEFENSE
3000 DEFENSE PENTAGON
WASHINGTON, DC 20301-3000

ACQUISITION
TECHNOLOGY
AND LOGISTICS

AUG 24 2010

Ms. Belva M. Martin
Acting Director, Acquisition and Sourcing Management
U.S. Government Accountability Office
441 G Street NW
Washington, DC 20548

Dear Ms. Martin:

This is the Department of Defense (DoD) response to the GAO draft report 10-523 "DEFENSE ACQUISITIONS: Navy's Ability to Overcome Challenges Facing the Littoral Combat Ship Will Determine Eventual Capabilities" dated June 30, 2010, (GAO Code 120834). Detailed comments on the report recommendations are enclosed.

The Department appreciates the opportunity to comment on the draft report. For further questions concerning this report, please contact Darlene Costello, Deputy Director, Naval Warfare, 703-697-2205.

Sincerely,

David G. Ahern
Director
Portfolio Systems Acquisition

Enclosure:
As stated

**GAO DRAFT REPORT DATED JUNE 30, 2010
GAO-10-523 (GAO CODE 120834)**

**"DEFENSE ACQUISITIONS: NAVY'S ABILITY TO OVERCOME
CHALLENGES FACING THE LITTORAL COMBAT SHIP WILL
DETERMINE EVENTUAL CAPABILITIES"**

**DEPARTMENT OF DEFENSE COMMENTS
TO THE GAO RECOMMENDATIONS**

RECOMMENDATION 1: The GAO recommends that the Secretary of Defense
ensure changes identified in building and testing the first four ships are
incorporated into the basic and functional design by the start of construction for
future Littoral Combat Ship (LCS) seaframes. (See page 36/GAO Draft Report.)

DoD RESPONSE: Concur. The Navy has been operating both LCS designs and
collecting design performance data. The Navy will continue to actively test and
report on ship performance as the first two follow ships are delivered and operated
in the Fleet so that the design performance of future ships is enhanced using
empirical data. The Fiscal Year (FY) 2010 solicitation uses the technical baseline
of the FY 2009 ships, plus known government directed changes, to establish a
stable baseline for the near term awards. The program can use existing ship and
class design services contracts to execute additional changes through the program's
formal configuration management process after contract award. The Department
also will review post-delivery test sequencing to ensure testing results can inform
future purchases as early as practicable.

RECOMMENDATION 2: The GAO recommends that the Secretary of Defense
update the LCS test and evaluation master plan to (1) account for any early
deployments of seaframes and the significant developmental challenges faced by
key mission package systems and (2) identify alternative approaches for
completing seaframe and mission package initial operational test and evaluation.
(See page 36/GAO Draft Report.)

DoD RESPONSE: Concur. The Navy will update the LCS Test and Evaluation
Master Plan (TEMP) after the down-select and the Milestone B decision to reflect
the changes in the program. The updated TEMP will reflect the new LCS
acquisition strategy approved in January 2010. In addition, it will address the test
and evaluation strategy of Developmental Testing (DT) and Operational Testing
(OT) for one mission package on each of the lead ships. This will support
achievement of initial operational capability as defined in the Flight 0 Capability

2

Development Document. The remaining LCS mission packages are scheduled for DT/OT on LCS 3, 4, and 5.

RECOMMENDATION 3: The GAO recommends that the Secretary of Defense update the LCS acquisition strategy to account for operational testing delays in the program and resequence planned purchases of ships and mission packages, as appropriate. (See page 36/GAO Draft Report.)

DoD RESPONSE: Concur. The Navy understands that alignment of the seaframe and mission modules production milestones must occur to meet requirements for initial operational test and evaluation and further production decisions. An updated schedule is under development. The Navy will continue to deliver LCS seaframes as currently planned and to field mission module capability in a spiral fashion as new systems are matured, tested, and accepted by the Fleet. In addition, the Department will review post-delivery test sequencing to ensure testing results can inform future purchases as early as practicable.

RECOMMENDATION 4: The GAO recommends that the Secretary of Defense ensure that future LCS cost estimates-including the program life cycle cost estimate currently planned for milestone B- are well-documented, comprehensive, accurate, and credible. (See page 37/GAO Draft Report.)

DoD RESPONSE: Concur. However, the cost analyses referenced in the draft GAO report were used to support investigatory trade studies and were not intended as a budget quality estimate, nor intended to inform contract negotiations. The estimate was developed to establish a cost baseline for the overall LCS program life cycle to be used as a point of departure for conducting cost trade-off analyses. In preparation for the program's Milestone B review, the Navy produced a complete cost estimate for the entire system lifecycle. This estimate fully incorporated cost estimating best practices, including cost risk, cost driver sensitivity analyses, and a fully documented Independent Cost Estimate (ICE), in accordance with NAVSEA 05C's 12-Step Cost Estimating Process. Additionally, NAVSEA 05C held discussions with OSD's Cost Assessment and Program Evaluation (CAPE) group. CAPE also prepared an ICE for the LCS program to support the Milestone B review.

Appendix IV: GAO Contact and Staff Acknowledgments

GAO Contact	Belva M. Martin, (202) 512-4841 or martinb@gao.gov
Acknowledgments	In addition to the contact named above, key contributors to this report were Karen Zuckerstein, Assistant Director; Greg Campbell; Christopher R. Durbin; Kristine Hassinger; Jeremy Hawk; Jasmin Jahanshahi; Julia P. Jebo; Jason Kelly; and Amber N. Keyser.

GAO's Mission	The Government Accountability Office, the audit, evaluation, and investigative arm of Congress, exists to support Congress in meeting its constitutional responsibilities and to help improve the performance and accountability of the federal government for the American people. GAO examines the use of public funds; evaluates federal programs and policies; and provides analyses, recommendations, and other assistance to help Congress make informed oversight, policy, and funding decisions. GAO's commitment to good government is reflected in its core values of accountability, integrity, and reliability.
Obtaining Copies of GAO Reports and Testimony	The fastest and easiest way to obtain copies of GAO documents at no cost is through GAO's Web site (www.gao.gov). Each weekday afternoon, GAO posts on its Web site newly released reports, testimony, and correspondence. To have GAO e-mail you a list of newly posted products, go to www.gao.gov and select "E-mail Updates."
Order by Phone	The price of each GAO publication reflects GAO's actual cost of production and distribution and depends on the number of pages in the publication and whether the publication is printed in color or black and white. Pricing and ordering information is posted on GAO's Web site, http://www.gao.gov/ordering.htm. Place orders by calling (202) 512-6000, toll free (866) 801-7077, or TDD (202) 512-2537. Orders may be paid for using American Express, Discover Card, MasterCard, Visa, check, or money order. Call for additional information.
To Report Fraud, Waste, and Abuse in Federal Programs	Contact: Web site: www.gao.gov/fraudnet/fraudnet.htm E-mail: fraudnet@gao.gov Automated answering system: (800) 424-5454 or (202) 512-7470
Congressional Relations	Ralph Dawn, Managing Director, dawnr@gao.gov, (202) 512-4400 U.S. Government Accountability Office, 441 G Street NW, Room 7125 Washington, DC 20548
Public Affairs	Chuck Young, Managing Director, youngc1@gao.gov, (202) 512-4800 U.S. Government Accountability Office, 441 G Street NW, Room 7149 Washington, DC 20548

www.ingramcontent.com/pod-product-compliance
Lightning Source LLC
Chambersburg PA
CBHW080607290526
45790CB00007B/2679